You + Me

Compiled by Dan Zadra & Kristel Wills
Designed by Sarah Forster
Created by Kobi Yamada

COMPENDIUM®
INCORPORATED

live inspired.

ACKNOWLEDGEMENTS

These quotations were gathered lovingly but unscientifically over several years and/or were contributed by many friends or acquaintances. Some arrived—and survived in our files—on scraps of paper and may therefore be imperfectly worded or attributed. To the authors, contributors and original sources, our thanks, and where appropriate, our apologies.
– The Editors

WITH SPECIAL THANKS TO

Jason Aldrich, Gerry Baird, Jay Baird, Neil Beaton, Josie Bissett, Jim and Alyssa Darragh & Family, Marta and Kyle Drevnia Jennifer and Matt Ellison & Family, Rob Estes, Michael and Leianne Flynn & Family, Jennifer Hurwitz, Heidi Jones, Carol A Kennedy, June Martin, Jessica Phoenix and Tom DesLongchamp, Steve and Janet Potter & Family, Diane Roger, Kirsten an Garrett Sessions, Andrea Shirley, Lin Smith, Clarie Yam and Erik Lee, Heidi Yamada & Family, Justi and Tote Yamada & Fam Bob and Val Yamada, Kaz and Kristin Yamada & Family, Tai and Joy Yamada, Anne Zadra, August and Arline Zadra, and Gu and Rosie Zadra.

CREDITS

Compiled by Dan Zadra & Kristel Wills
Designed by Sarah Forster
Created by Kobi Yamada

ISBN: 978-1-932319-59-0

HAPPINESS was made to be SHARED.

+ JEAN RACINE

Someone said that love is blind, but that's not really true. Shakespeare had it right when he wrote, "Love adds a precious seeing to the eye." In fact, love is the only thing that lets us see all the possibilities in life and each other with crystal clarity.

Love looks beyond our limitations and illuminates the gifts that no one else had looked quite far enough to find. It helps us discover qualities in ourselves that we didn't even know were missing. With love we feed each other's dreams and share each other's joys and sorrows.

The best part is that sharing life actually makes life bigger. True love is never about what we take from each other, it's always about what we give to each other. As Kathleen Norris reminds us, "Anything, everything, little or big becomes an adventure when the right person shares it."

I come
to fetch
MY HEART
where I left it,
that is to say,
in YOURS.

+ JULIETTE DROUET

YOU and LOVE came into my life
at the very SAME MOMENT.

+ UNKNOWN

when
you APPEARED
all that was thought to
be LOST was
suddenly
FOUND.

+ FRANCISCO

I have LEARNED not to worry about love,
but to HONOR its coming with all MY HEART.

 ALICE WALKER

You have to WALK CAREFULLY in the beginning of love; the RUNNING across fields into your lover's arms can only come LATER when you're SURE they won't laugh if you trip.

+ JONATHAN CARROLL

Sometimes
your NEARNESS
takes my breath away.

And all the things I want to say can find no voice.

Then in SILENCE, I can only hope,
my EYES will speak
MY HEART.

+ UNKNOWN

smitten

In your presence
I fell more in love with
the BEST OF MYSELF.
That was your gift.

+ WILLIAM CUMMINGS

EVERYONE
carries
with them at least
ONE PIECE
to someone ELSE'S
PUZZLE.

✛ LAWRENCE KUSHNER

Love's greatest GIFT is its ability to make everything it touches SACRED.

+ BARBARA DE ANGELIS

Turn to the MIRACLE next to you.

+ HAL EDWARDS

laugh
together
want
Devotion
friend forever
beautiful
side by side
sacred
VALU
fun
thrive
spontaneity
fire
loves
smile

Spark Desire

When you lov'd me, and I lov'd you,
then BOTH of us were BORN ANEW.

+ SAMUEL TAYLOR COLERIDGE

In love, ONE and ONE are ONE. + JEAN-PAUL SARTRE

TRUE
LOVE
is when
your HEART
and your MIND are saying
the SAME
THING.

+ LEANNA L. BARTRA

A love that DEFIES all logic is sometimes
the most LOGICAL thing in the world.

+ ANONYMOUS

When **ONE** loves somebody
everything is clear—where
TO GO, what **TO DO**—it all
TAKES CARE OF ITSELF
and one doesn't have to ask
anybody about anything.

+ MAKSIM GORKY

True LOVE
and
FRIENDSHIP
are the SAME.

+ JAMES THOMSON

Be a FRIEND, the rest will follow.

+ EMILY DICKINSON

There isn't a PARTICLE of you that I don't
KNOW, REMEMBER, and WANT.

+ NOEL COWARD

They gave each other a SMILE with a FUTURE in it.

+ RING LARDNER

takes my
breath
away
takes my breath
away
takes my
breath
aw

nome

With a KISS let us set out for an unknown WORLD.

+ ALFRED DE MUSSET

We LOVE because it is the
ONLY true ADVENTURE.

+ NIKKI GIOVANNI

warmth

Love is EVERYTHING it's cracked up to be.
That's why people are so cynical about it…
It really *is* worth FIGHTING for, being
BRAVE for, RISKING everything for.

+ ERICA JONG

Love,

YOU KNOW,

seeks to make HAPPY

rather than

to be HAPPY.

+ CHARLES WILLIAM GORDON

Loving is not just CARING DEEPLY,
it's, above all, UNDERSTANDING.

+ FRANCOISE SAGAN

I did not hear the WORDS you said, instead I heard the LOVE.

+ MIGUEL DE CERVANTES

The quarrels of lovers are like SUMMER STORMS.
Everything is more beautiful when they have PASSED.

+ SUZANNE NECKER

The
ULTIMATE
TEST OF A
relationship is to
disagree
but to
HOLD hands.

+ ALEXANDRA PENNEY

There is a **STAGE** with people we love when we are no longer separate from them…We push back **OUR** hair because **THEIRS** is in their eyes.

+ NAN FAIRBROTHER

It's a UNIQUE relationship.
We share a SOUL. We live
in a special place. We thrive
on combined SPIRIT.

+ SARA CORPENING

Sweetheart

Where you love SOMEBODY a whole lot, and you know that person LOVES YOU, that's the MOST BEAUTIFUL place in the world.

+ ANN CAMERON

Find the ONE who makes your heart SMILE.

+ UNKNOWN

All you need
IN THE WORLD
is love
AND LAUGHTER.

That's all anybody needs.

To have LOVE
IN ONE hand
AND
LAUGHTER IN THE OTHER.

+ AUGUST WILSON

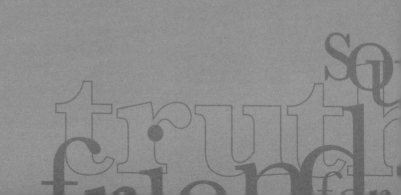

The MORE I know you,
the more I WANT to know YOU more.

+ ROY LESSIN

It is a HAPPY CHANCE if we, changing, continue to love a CHANGED person.

+ W. SOMERSET MAUGHAM

Love, the magician, knows this little
trick whereby TWO PEOPLE walk
in DIFFERENT directions yet always
remain SIDE BY SIDE.

+ HUGH PRATHER

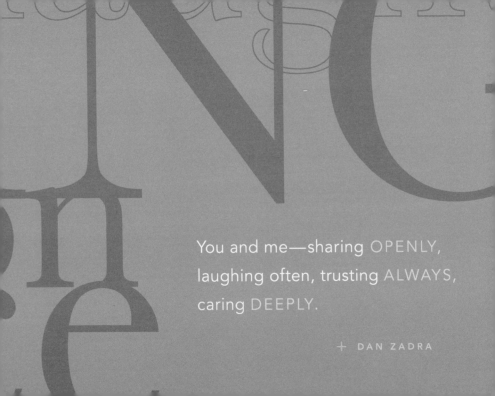

You and me—sharing OPENLY,
laughing often, trusting ALWAYS,
caring DEEPLY.

+ DAN ZADRA

I think we DREAM so we don't have to be apart...If we're in EACH OTHER'S DREAMS, we can be TOGETHER all the time.

+ THOMAS HOBBES

feel hope honor

In DREAMS
and in LOVE,
there are
no
IMPOSSIBILITIES.

+ JÁNOS ARANY

True love:
long SOUGHT, rarely FOUND,
and forever KEPT.

+ PAT COLLELO